# Test Requirement Driven Development

# Test Requirement Driven Development

## *The product development catalyst*

Michael O'Reilly

To

Sarah for love, faith, devotion, and perseverance;

Liam, Skylar, and Seamus for inspiration;

and

Nick Porzio, my godfather and lifelong source of aspiration.

# CONTENTS

# ACKNOWLEDGMENTS

This work is the culmination of years of effort, discussion, head scratching, and delightful insight of how product-development teams and individuals can work more effectively to produce an outstanding product. To those individuals with whom I shared my working hours, I thank you for your contributions and continued friendship.

Besides my family, whom I acknowledge in the dedication, two other individuals have been instrumental in convincing me to put this methodology in print. Frank Frazier and David Sallet shared with me the benefits Test Requirement Driven Development can provide and were gracious enough to provide feedback as I assembled years of notes and discussions into this book. Over many lunches and dinners, they convinced me that there is no better time than the present to share this new way of building products. Thanks, fellas. You're the best!

# INTRODUCTION

Talent, teamwork, and "beginning with the end in mind."

On September 19, 2010, in Gillette Stadium at Foxboro, Massachusetts, the Green Bay Packers, having just scored, kicked off to the home team New England Patriots. With two minutes and seventeen seconds remaining in the second quarter, the Packers didn't want to take a chance of the Patriots scoring a touchdown off the kickoff. So instead of kicking the ball deep to the Patriots' speedy kickoff return player, Sammy Morris, they opted to kick the ball low to the ground, where it skipped and bounced into the hands of Dan Connolly, who was standing on the Patriots' twenty-five yard line.

In 2010, Dan Connolly was a 6' 4", 314-pound offensive lineman for the New England Patriots. As an offensive lineman, his specialty was blocking defenders so that running backs could run the ball or the quarterback had enough time to throw the ball to wide receivers. Connolly began that season as a reserve player, not a starter. The team recognized his talent, and he was selected to participate on special teams. Special teams are an assembly of players who have great talent. Though they may not have a starting position, they are called upon for special situations such as kickoff opportunities. As the Patriots' preseason concluded, through a combination of his hard work, other players' contract issues, and injuries to his teammates, Dan found himself as a starting offensive lineman, as well as a special-team player.

As the football bounced and weaved in his direction, Dan secured it in his massive arms, put his head down, and ran like heck toward the goal line. As he rumbled up field toward the goal line, he was able to shake off a few Green Bay defenders. Dan moved diagonally along the left sideline, but he was far from being the speediest player on the field. The Packer players quickly caught up to the Patriots lineman, ready to bring him down. However, Dan's teammates, sharing his goal and passion to score a touchdown for the team, came to his rescue. Safety Sergio Brown, running back Sammy Morris, and defensive linebacker Rob Ninkovich threw blocks against the Green Bay players chasing down Connolly. The play ended with Connolly tackled on the Green Bay four yard line. He had brought his team within twelve feet of the goal line. Seventy-one yards from where he first touched the ball, he was surrounded by his celebrating teammates. The first teammates to congratulate Dan were the ones who were on the field with him—the special team players.

So why would a book about product- and software-development methodologies discuss the feat of a lifetime of an NFL player?

Because Dan Connolly's action embodies the essence of what Test Requirement Driven Development (TREDD) is about. It places a focus on quality, a "beginning with end in mind" attitude, and allows members of a product development team make improvements toward delivering a quality product that are rooted in what they can contribute based on their talents and experience, and not limited to their role. Too many times product development teams become fiefdoms of specialties, where only those members who are part a particular subgroup of the team can make a contribution in that area. Frequently, this parochial expertise monopoly has a negative impact on product quality and cost, project schedule, and product features. It destroys the collective strength an organization was looking to leverage when it assembled the product development team.

As an offensive lineman, Dan Connolly did not spend his time at practice training on how the run past defenders. But when he picked up the football on the Patriots' twenty-five yard line, no one on his team said he wasn't supposed to run with the ball. Dan had talent, and his team didn't inhibit him from making a contribution. Just the opposite. They endorsed his opportunity to contribute. They used their talents to help the team score a touchdown, supporting Dan Connolly's determined effort.

As you read this book, which outlines a new methodology for developing product you will see several references to software development since my background is in developing software products. However, having described this methodology to others, I see no reason why it cannot be applied to various types of development efforts. As a result, the team developing the product is not referred to as a software development team, although the team members are found in typical software development projects. Rather the team developing the product is described as the **product development team**. In the Agile methodology, the product development team is similar to the SCRUM team. Regardless of the terminology, this collection of talent is responsible for developing a superb product that will be used by a targeted consumer audience.

Test Requirement Driven Development will not by itself make any project an immediate success. TREDD is a methodology that, if applied properly, will allow a product development team to reap multiple benefits, which in turn will help them work more efficiently. With this efficiency, the organization can manage costs and scheduling better, and enjoy the benefit of new opportunities generated from the product development team.

Since it is a methodology, it will not solve organizational issues beyond its scope. Likewise, Test Requirement Driven Development can only be as successful as the organization's commitment to providing qualified staff and endorsing the product development team with the support and confidence it needs to execute its tasks in the manner the Test Requirement Driven Development methodology outlines. After all, it is the staff of an organization that makes the product. They are the differentiator that TREDD catalyzes toward higher effectiveness.

Be open for a new paradigm. Embrace the change. Enjoy the success!

# 1. ORIGINS

It was bad. It was real bad.

The team had been working on the project for over eight months and still had nothing substantial to show for its efforts. People had come and gone from the project, some with strong abilities, others with little confidence that the project they were working on was going to be successful or worth their while. For the next four weeks, I had the benefit of being the outside observer: listening in on daily SCRUM standup meetings (fifteen-minute sessions during which all team members state what they did the day before, what they planned on doing that day, and what impediments they faced to move their work toward conclusion); meeting with team members; evaluating the product; and looking at the project schedule, including the burndown chart (a Scrum work cycle monitoring tool).[1]

As I observed the team dynamics, several factors became apparent. First, the team's velocity (speed at which they built functionality) was not very fast at all. In fact, it was going in a negative direction, meaning they were falling behind the schedule they had all committed to management and the product owner (the individual who had the vision and the responsibility for delivering a product that satisfied the stakeholder's needs). Instead of building new functionality, the team was working exclusively on repairing defects found by the testing team.

Second, interactions between team members were filled with tension and distrust. The daily standup meetings would quickly

---

[1] Ken Schwaber and Mike Beedle, *"Agile Software Development with Scrum"*, (Saddle River: Prentice Hall, 2002), pg. 40-45

devolve into defect reviews. The testing group (QA members) would provide a status for defects they had found the prior day, indicating which previously existing ones had been fixed and which were still broken. Then the engineers would announce which defects from the prior day were done and ready for the testing group to reverify. The testing group would say it had found additional defects, some new and some that had been working properly but were now broken. The interchange between both groups would spiral down to a tone of mutual frustration by the meeting's conclusion. The team agreed to continue to work hard resolving all defects that were considered major, critical, or a blocker.

Lastly, there was no well-organized plan that could reliably forecast when the development effort would be complete, other than when all defects in the major, critical, or blocker categories were found and resolved. This third factor led the team toward accepting the concept that their sole purpose was to resolve defects. The team didn't dare to consider why its product quality was so poor. The product manager couldn't project a timeline because no one knew how many defects would be found during the next testing effort. The testing group kept revisiting their testing plan, over and over again.

Management became more concerned since it had revenue projections and client commitments based upon the product features that were being developed; by that time over a $1 million had been invested in product development. The product milestone dates, defined by management and agreed to by the product development team, were not met. The dates were recast as the product development team predicted with high confidence that the new dates would be met. Although management was aware that the team was not delivering as expected, it didn't know that the team's negative velocity would make it impossible to meet the production timelines. The investment being applied to the initiative was no way near the projected financial return.

The product development team was so busy trying to fix existing defects, they weren't able to begin other development tasks that were scheduled. Even worse, the team had no time to evaluate its performance and make adjustments so that the product could be developed better and delivered in the scheduled timeframe.

The situation I've described is not unique. It occurs in many organizations striving to produce new products. It continues to occur today and may be what your organization is facing currently.

Even though this product development team was following an Agile approach, it lacked three key elements:

- commitment to quality

- accountability

- trustful collaboration

The product development team required a methodology that would give priority to each of these aspects. It needed a methodology that required all team members to deliver quality contributions in developing the product. And the contributions they made needed to be transparent for all to see. They needed a methodology that did not leave the QA members of the team feeling as if they were being placed in the difficult position of verifying and approving the product on the eve of the delivery date.

A methodology was needed to ensure each team member was accountable for the work he or she passed forward to another team member. One that allowed team members to make contributions and work closer with each other in order to complete the product functionality within each product development life cycle. Lastly, a methodology that persistently supported the team to focus on the deliverables for each product development life cycle, and that clearly evaluated the strengths and weaknesses of team members during each life cycle, so that the product development team constantly evolved with greater effectiveness.

Realizing the need to help product development teams perform more effectively, I created **Test Requirement Driven Development** methodology.    Its demonstrated benefits are improved team morale, increased product quality, support of reliable product delivery schedules, and costs control.

# 2. DEFINING TREDD

Test **RE**quirement **D**riven **D**evelopment (TREDD) is a development methodology geared to enhance the capability of a product development team to deliver quality product features in their entirety by the end of each product development life cycle (For those using Scrum, this would be a Sprint).[2] Regardless if the product development life cycle is seven days, fourteen days, twenty-eight days, or more, Test Requirement Driven Development provides focus that allows each member to contribute his or her talents to his specific area of expertise, as well as engaging any ancillary talents to help other product development team members to complete their product development life cycle deliverables. Along with promoting product development team talents, TREDD places a strong emphasis on collaborative team dynamics and the quest for quality. Quality effort for the product development team is measured through the development and maturation of *test requirements*, which will be described in further detail shortly. By utilizing the analysis of specific metrics generated from the test requirements, TREDD allows product development teams and management to identify what corrective actions may be required to enhance the product development team's operating effectiveness.

TREDD originated in the development of software products for large, medium, and small companies. The companies varied in their market segment, but their need to improve the effectiveness of their product development teams was consistent.

---

[2] KenSchwaber," *Agile Project Management with Scrum*", (Redmond: Microsoft Press, 2004), pg. 8.

Consequently, Test Requirement Driven Development can be applied to any company, regardless of its size or market segment. And although its beginnings are founded in software engineering, its principles resonate with other operational groups.

Software development organizations typically execute some form of product development methodology. Some use Waterfall or Rational Unified Process (RUP), and others some form of Agile development such as SCRUM. The principles of TREDD can be applied to some degree against several development methodologies. However, its most successful implementations have been with the Agile development methodology, SCRUM. In the following pages, this Agile methodology will be used as an example framework to illustrate how TREDD can be implemented.

## Warning Signs of Ineffective Product Development

When product development teams begin to lose effectiveness, several warning signs appear. For software development projects, these signs can be:

- ✓ missed deliverable dates

- ✓ increased defects

- ✓ growing backlog of undelivered functionality

- ✓ escalating project costs

- ✓ decaying of the team's interpersonal working relationships

Many companies face this erosion of product development team effectiveness some time during their existence. For some companies, this is an unpleasant recurrence. What these companies require, and perhaps what your company may be seeking at this moment, is a way to restore the product development team's effectiveness to a point where the team can recover and produce at not just 100 percent efficiency, but go beyond 100 percent. The pathway to increased performance will require:

- a process that reinforces quality effort,
- transparent view of individual team member's contributions,
- simple metrics that objectively measure the product development team's performance,
- management support to implement a quality centered collaborative product development methodology.

Test Requirement Driven Development provides an opportunity to allow these four performances attributes, which are essential for highly effective product development teams, to flourish.

## TREDD vs. TDD vs. ATDD

As we begin to define Test Requirement Driven Development, it is worthwhile to note the similarities and differences TREDD has with Test Driven Development (TDD) and with Acceptance Test Driven Development (ATDD).[3] From a software development perspective, the essential element of TDD is the creation of unit tests that are coded and can be executed with automated testing. Specifically during life cycles when a software system has been

---

[3] Beck, Kent, *"Test Driven Development: by Example"*, (Boston: Pearson Education, Inc., 2003) pg. 11. Larman, Craig and Vodde, Bas, *"Acceptance Test-Driven Development with Robot Framework"*,  Version 1.1: pg. 1.

modified and rebuilt, the TDD discipline of creating code with unit tests provides a safety net of cross-checks, ensuring that updates to software do not break existing or ancillary functionality, which can be detected at the code level by way of the software engineering unit tests.

Test Requirement Driven Development, being a rapid-development methodology, wholeheartedly embraces TDD. It is a best practice that will improve the overall quality of the product being developed. TREDD differs from TDD because its focus is on the creation of test requirements that can be executed and verified by the product development team, as well as using metrics to improve the product development team's performance. TDD activity may be a test requirement, where members of the product development team verify the existence and execution of well-formed TDD unit tests.

Acceptance Test Driven Development (ATDD) is similar to the test-requirment processes TREDD uses. Both methodologies favor bringing the acceptance tests to the beginning of the development cycle. TREDD, however, places a greater emphasis on encouraging the entire product development team to participate in the creation and evaluation of the test requirements. Additionally, TREDD places importance on the need for the product development team to persistently produce quality products through outstanding contributions. The ability to measure quality, as will be shown later on, is achieved through analysis of the test requirement during the product-development lifecycle.

## TREDD Objective

TREDD has an overarching objective to provide and/or supplement an existing methodology, allowing the product development team to attain greater results by:

- utilizing test requirements to simplify the product-development process,

- leveraging test requirements results to address quality and increase product development team effectiveness,

- endorsing a high collaboration and creative atmosphere to enhance the talents of the product development team.

Let's see how TREDD achieves these results.

# 3. TEST REQUIREMENTS

**Illustrative Product Development Team**

To help demonstrate how TREDD can be applied, let's create a fictional product development team that can be used and referenced throughout for illustrative purposes. As you review each role defined in Table 1 below, keep in mind how these roles may relate to the roles within a product development team in your own organization.

TABLE 1. Product Development Team Roles

| ROLE | RESPONSIBILITY |
|------|----------------|
| Product Owner | Define the vision of the product, prioritize work for the product development team, provide feedback during development, responsible for final decisions to accept or reject the final product |
| Product Management (aka business analyst) | Works with other organizational members to define detailed specifications for the targeted product functionality being developed |
| Development | Responsible for actually producing the product. (i.e., software engineers) |
| Quality Assurance | Will test delivered product functionality, reporting all defects. Responsible for signing off that the product is ready to be released to the consumer |

## QA Members Under Pressure

In my observations of product-development life cycles across numerous companies, two critical characteristics stand out pertaining to the interaction of QA members. These characteristics can result in the product development team losing effectiveness.

The first characteristic of low effectiveness occurs when defects are discovered and the product is sent back to the development members for reengineering.  Following corrective actions, the revised product is returned to QA members for validation. If the product being developed is of poor quality, each cycle of *defect detection-defect correction* may provide fertile ground for animosity and tension to grow between with the development and QA members.  QA members can feel that the product they are evaluating was created with little regard to quality or with a low appreciation for the effort QA members have to expend to validate product functionality as created by development members.

From another perspective, development members can become agitated when additional defects are discovered.  Many of the defects are product features identified by QA members through their experience and in their interpretation of the requirements, which QA members feel confident the consumer will expect.  The development members sometimes feel the additional requirements from QA members are not needed or are obscure.

The second characteristic of low effectiveness that impacts QA members is the increased pressure placed upon them at the end of the product-development life cycle.  Especially when the product development team is inefficient, the deliverables for the product seldom reach the QA members until near the end of the product-development life cycle; that is, near the product delivery date.  This latency has a negative effect on the QA members who now must exert extra effort, in most cases within a time frame only a fraction of what they originally had planned for. Additionally, and arguably most importantly, the overall quality of the product is jeopardized. Since all resources are working beyond their normal productivity zones to meet the product delivery time frame, undesirable defects can be overlooked and placed into production for the consumer to unpleasantly discover.

From these observations the following becomes clear:

- The collaborative dynamics that were sought in assembling the product development team erode as the cycle of *defect detection-defect correction* spirals throughout the product development life cycle, eroding the relationship between the development and QA members.

- The pressure placed upon the QA members is detrimental to the quality of the product being produced.

## Rise of the Test Requirement

To address these issues, something needs to change. At the end of the product-development life cycle, the product is ready for the consumer only after QA members are not able to find any defects that would be deemed unacceptable by the consumer. The product development team fully accepts and understands this principle. QA members define and develop testing criteria, which we will refer to as test cases, based upon their review and interpretation of product requirements and specifications, written or otherwise considered. Given this fact for final product approval of the product, one clear question arises: Why aren't the criteria that the QA members are using to determine if the product is ready for the consumer shared with the development members?

Reviewing the roles of the product development team within the product development life cycle, there is no clear reason to prevent the test cases from being used earlier in the product-development life cycle.  As a consequence, a new paradigm is formed for the *test requirement*.  Leveraging the high value that the test case has to the final product definition, its prominence in the early stages of the product-development life cycle, it is no longer just a task to "test the quality of the product."  Rather it is now given the recognition for what it has been all along, namely the requirements that the product has to satisfy for the consumer to be pleased with it.  Enter the *test requirement*.

# *TEST CASE*

## +

## *REQUIREMENTS*

## = **TEST REQUIREMENT**

## Test Requirement Details

The main conduit for quality, the test case, that was previously defined and executed by the Quality Assurance members is now given prominence throughout the product development team as test requirements.

### Pass or Fail Aspect

The product development team will use test requirements to define, develop, and validate the functionality of the product being produced. Test requirements are created with a precise *pass or fail* aspect. This means that each individual product requirement can be seen in the product (pass) or not (fail). They are distinctive, singular requirements that define how the product functionality is to behave. By embracing this concept, the test case becomes a requirement.

### QA Makes Contributions Early

Test requirements provide their maximum value when they are defined and made available to the product development team early in the product-development life cycle. QA members, instead of holding onto and applying their knowledge and expectations of how the product should behave at the end of that life cycle, are now expected to bring their valuable contributions to the beginning of the lifecycle for the entire product development team to consider, apply, and benefit from. If the development of test requirements lags slightly behind in terms of product-development timeline expectations, product development can and should proceed while test requirements are being created— as long as there exists a well-formed consensus of how the product should be developed among the product development team members. This means that product development is in alignment to the test requirements being generated. For this rapid development to be successful, clear, continual communication needs to take place among all product-development team members.

## Test Requirement Contributors

Test requirements can be defined and supplied by any member of the product development team. In typical product development teams, product management (some may refer to these members as business analysts) have the most availability and directive to create product requirements. With the elemental structure and *pass or fail* nature of test requirements, the QA members are also encouraged—in fact are expected—to play a large role in defining the test requirements. Other members of the product development team are encouraged to contribute test requirements when they see it will add value to the product function being developed.

## Test Requirements Align to the User Story

An important component of test requirements is aligning a given product functionality with the scope of what the product development team had agreed to undertake. If Agile is the development methodology being used, this means that the test requirement has to encompass an element of functionality that satisfies the user story (a brief summary of the user's expectations of system functionality). The user story gives the test requirement context. It provides scope and boundary for the product functionality being developed, so the product development team can determine if the test requirement is appropriate. When the test requirement is defined, the entire team will have access to it.   If product development team members feel that the test requirement is not appropriate for the user story, they can discuss its worthiness with the originator of the test requirement and, if necessary, with other product development team members or the author of the user story.  If the test requirement doesn't have merit, it will be removed and declared out of scope.  If it is valid, the test requirement will be worked on by the product development team as part of the product functionality as defined by the user story.

For example, if the user story is defined as *paint the shed*, then a test requirement of *butter the popcorn at the theater* would quite obviously be rejected as not within the spirit or scope of the user story.

## Test Requirement Example Using Agile

Let's take a look at how test requirements add value during the development of a product.  We will compare the life cycle of a particular product feature developed using an Agile methodology, and then integrate the test requirement as TREDD would expect it to be applied.  In this scenario, a software company is creating a data-entry screen that includes the ability for the consumer to enter a zip code.

### Scenario 1: Zip Code Entry

A product team is asked to develop a data-entry screen that will process the input of an address for a consumer.   In this scenario we will focus specifically on the *zip code* field of the address.

Using Agile, a user story could be defined as follows:

*As a consumer I want to submit a zip code as part my address.*

For the given user story, there may be one or more acceptance criteria statements associated with the zip-code field.[4]  Let's provide some acceptance criteria so that the development members can begin creating a data-entry screen that captures a zip code.

- System will accept 5 characters for the zip-code field

- System will accept not accept zip + 4 zip-code entries

- System will not allow zip codes greater than 5 characters

- System will display error message at top of the screen when zip-code edits fail

With the user story and acceptance criteria defined, the development members of the product development team begin coding the new screen and zip-code field.   After a short

---

[4] Acceptance Criteria are statements that provide additional detail and understanding to the development team of how the requested product functionality should behave within scope of the user story.

time (since they are top-notch engineers), they have fully built the requested zip-code entry field, based on the user story and acceptance criteria. They have even completed tests to make sure it is working as the consumer would expect it to! Those tests are:

- Zip code with 5 characters, numeric of course, are accepted and stored in the database

- Zip code less than 5 characters produce an error message at the top of the screen stating "Some error will show here"

- Zip code field with 5 characters plus dash plus 4 more characters are not allowed to be entered into the zip-code field.  Maximum field size is 5 characters.

Meanwhile ... the QA members have been busy in their spare time creating test cases to verify the zip-code field is working as they would expect the consumer to interact with it.  They developed eleven test cases that are required to pass in order for the product feature to be certified as ready for the consumer to use in production:

1. Successfully accept 5 numeric values entered into the zip-code field.

2.  Successfully store in the database 5 numeric values that were entered into the zip-code field.

3.  Verify error message appears on line 2 of the screen stating Invalid Zip Code when fewer than 5 numeric values are entered.

4.  Verify error message appears on line 2 of the screen stating Invalid Zip Code when a value containing 5 of the same numbers is entered.

5.  Verify data field for the zip code prevents alphabetical characters from being entered; does not require an error message to be displayed.

6.  Verify data field for the zip code prevents more than 5 numeric values from being entered; does not require an error message to be displayed.

7.  Verify data field for the zip code prevents all special characters (i.e., $, %, #) from being entered; does not require an error message to be displayed.

8.  Verify that special characters cannot be pasted (control + *v*) into the zip-code field.

9.  If the zip-code field is blank when the submit screen button is selected, verify the standard zip-code-error message appears.

10. If zip-code field has fewer than 5 characters when the submit screen button is selected, verify the standard zip-code-error message appears.

11. If zip-code-error message is present, it is removed after a valid zip code is entered.

This level of definition is what most Agile product development groups would expect to see during the elaboration of a particular product function.  It is lean, direct, and action orientated, and provides a great vision of what capabilities the requested functionality may possess.  The additional details describing product functionality are just not available in acceptance criteria. They are most often found in the test cases generated by the QA members.

### Putting Test Requirements into Action

Using the zip-code product feature as described in scenario 1, let's see how TREDD, using test requirements, allows the product development team to develop the zip-code functionality better than traditional Agile.

**TABLE 2.** Traditional Agile and TREDD Comparison

| | Traditional Agile | TREDD |
|---|---|---|
| **Scope** | USER STORY<br><br>*As a consumer I want to submit a zip code so my address has this value.* | USER STORY<br><br>*As a consumer I want to submit a zip code so my address has this value.* |
| **Criteria** | ACCEPTANCE CRITERIA<br><br>1. *System will accept 5 characters for the zip-code field.*<br><br>2. *System will not accept zip + 4 zip code entries.*<br><br>3. *System will not allow zip codes greater than 5 characters.*<br><br>4. *System will display error message at top of the screen when zip code edits fail.* | TEST REQUIREMENTS<br><br>1. *Successfully accept 5 numeric values entered into the zip-code field.*<br><br>2. *Successfully store in the database 5 numeric values that were entered into the zip-code field.*<br><br>3. *Verify error message appears on line 2 of the screen stating Invalid Zip Code when fewer than 5 numeric values are entered.*<br><br>4. *Verify error message appears on line 2 of the screen stating Invalid Zip Code when a value containing 5 of the same numbers is entered.*<br><br>5. *Verify data field for the zip code prevents alphabetical characters from being entered; does not require an error message to be displayed.* |

| | Traditional Agile | TREDD |
|---|---|---|
| | | 6. *Verify data field for the zip code prevents more than 5 numeric values from being entered; does not require an error message to be displayed.* |
| | | 7. *Verify data field for the zip code prevents all special characters (i.e., $, %, #) from being entered; does not require an error message to be displayed.* |
| | | 8. *Verify that special characters cannot be pasted (control + v) into the zip-code field.* |
| | | 9. *If the zip-code field is blank when the submit screen button is selected, verify the standard zip-code-error message appears.* |
| | | 10. *If zip-code field has fewer than 5 characters when the submit screen button is selected, verify the standard zip-code-error message appears.* |
| | | 11. *Verify prior zip-code-error message is removed when a valid zip code is entered.* |

As shown in table 2, when compared to traditional Agile, TREDD's increased specification for the development of the zip-code field is quite remarkable—eleven test requirements versus just four acceptance-criteria statements.

## Effort Impact

When we compare the significant increase in specification between traditional Agile and TREDD with its test requirements, clearly more effort is being expended on requirements in the early stages of the product life cycle to obtain the level of detail and consideration that the QA members generate for their test cases. Agile encourages providing enough documentation to support the needs of the product being produced. TREDD also embraces this principle of minimal documentation. In reviewing the level of requirement details as shown in table 1, it appears that TREDD is adding more documentation than traditional Agile.

On the surface this appears to be true. However, what TREDD is really doing is taking the test cases that the QA members created and planned to use during their verification of product functionality, which typically occurs at the end of the product-development life cycle, and brings them forward to the beginning of the cycle. Even with traditional Agile, the test cases have always existed. However, they were kept within the domain of the QA members. These test cases are required to pass in order for the product to be considered worthy of presenting to the consumer. *So the effort to produce the test requirements is not an additional burden to the product development team. It is simply a resequencing of activity.*

## Increase Product Development Team Efficiency & Velocity

Now that we have shifted the contributions of the QA members with their test cases from the end of the product-development life cycle toward the beginning, the product development team is positioned to use its collective talents to increase efficiency and thereby increase the velocity of work being produced for each product-development life cycle.

The presence of the fully visible and accessible test requirements in the beginning phases of the product-development life cycle has the following benefits:

- provides the product development team greater insight into the final requirements for the product,
- enables the development members to have a wider understanding of the functions they are responsible to build,
- allows product development team members to add and/or refine the product functionality quickly and easily from a single source,
- provides a foundation for tests the development members are expected to execute to ensure that the product has been created properly and with quality before QA members verify product functionality.

This last point is most essential to TREDD.  Since development members now have an understanding of how the product should perform,  which can be determined as acceptable or not in a *pass or fail* evaluation via the test requirement, those members are provided with a vehicle to ensure their code is of quality and working correctly.  This means that, barring any deltas due to testing data or changes as the product moves into a new environment (i.e., a development environment to a test environment), code that is not working when evaluated by the QA members is a result of the development members not producing a quality product. When that occurs, the product development team can take corrective actions as needed to raise quality. QA members are now truly validating proven functionality, rather than looking at an untested product feature deliverable.

As stated previously, the TREDD test requirements shift the effort of the QA members toward the front of the product life cycle. Their effort is not diminished. So where does the product development team gain velocity?

The product development team gains velocity with three immediate savings:

1. Specifications are consolidated into the test requirement. *Product management and QA members are combining instead of duplicating their efforts* in defining the product specifications by way of the test requirement.

2. Development members are producing higher-quality product due to the test requirement. They have greater insight into all of the required product functionality. They have a clear list of tests that the product feature being created must satisfy.

3. QA members are now receiving a product that has already been through a round of acceptance criteria tests. QA members are expected to execute the same tests in an *acceptance* environment. Since the first round of testing is being performed by development members during the creation of the product feature, which is equal to efforts of the QA members' *acceptance* testing, the chances of defects being found by QA members is greatly diminished. As a result, the iterations of *defect detection-defect correction* have been greatly reduced. This results in the product development team completing the product-development life cycle on or very close to the scheduled

completion date, and potentially completing more work each iteration.

# 4. ENHANCING QUALITY AND PRODUCTIVITY

## Measuring Product Development Efficiency

Test Requirement Driven Development provides an outstanding opportunity to measure a product development team's efficiency. This can provide the organization with the ability to determine which product development teams are performing with high efficiency and which teams need assistance.

The ability to measure the efficiency of a product development team is where TREDD differs significantly from traditional Agile and Waterfall methodologies. Using the results of these measurements will allow the organization and product development teams to make any adjustments needed to improve performance.

Finding this critical information requires the product development team to classify a key data point—the test requirement state. Specifically, if the test requirement passed or failed during the evaluation by the QA members, or if it was rejected and deemed out of scope for the product-development life cycle. This measurement of the test requirement provides a clear and objective measurement of the product development team's performance, rather than relying on measured velocity or subjective opinion alone.[5]

---

[5] Velocity is a SCRUM term which is the average the number of hours or story points a SCRUM team completes over several development iterations.

## Classifying Test Requirements Results

The status of test requirements is the pulse of the product development process. If tracked and analyzed properly, they will provide management and the product development team with a clear understanding of how well the product life cycle is being executed and how effective the team is in building a quality product.

Analyzing and reporting test requirements during the product-development life cycle requires classifying test requirements results into four categories:

- Passed Test Requirements (PTR)

- New Test Requirements (NTR)

- Defective Test Requirements (DTR)

- Rejected Test Requirements (RTR)

Let's look more closely at how analyzing and taking action on the test-requirement results contributes to the success and increased efficiency of the product development team.

### *Passed Test Requirements (PTR)*

Passed test requirements (PTR) are test requirements that have successfully passed verification by the development and QA members. The product development team's goal is to generate a high percentage of PTRs; close to 100 percent. Everyone on the product development team should be focused on achieving this goal. If this goal is reached, it means all the test requirements defined for a given product feature (or user story, if Agile is used) have successfully passed QA's test efforts. In other words, the product has been developed to satisfy the test requirements and, as a result, meet the consumers' expectations. The organization should positively reward the product development team because they utilized maximum efficiency in developing the product (assuming they did so in a timely manner). The investment of the product being developed is optimized.

Test requirement results other than PTR or high-value New Test Requirements (NTR) mean that the team is losing efficiency and in most cases velocity. The team is either doing more work than it should or work that is required is being omitted. As a result the organization is losing money and time developing its product due to inefficiency.

### New Test Requirements (NTR)

New test requirements (NTR) are requirements that were discovered after development of the product functionality began and were not identified in the initial list of test requirements. NTRs identified after QA members have completed their verification and provided their approval of developed functionality would belong to a new user story, since the original user story has been completed and all test requirements for that user story have been satisfied.

NTRs can be both a benefit and a determent. In the spirit of iterative development, new requirements that help make the product better and are in alignment with the new product function should be identified, defined, and applied to the product functionality that is being developed—as long as the product development team agrees to take on the development effort.

This is important because the decision to include this development may have an impact on the product development team's resources. TREDD encourages the product development team to have a strong sense of empowerment and ownership for the product functionality they are producing. Therefore it is the responsibility of the product development team to determine if the NTR should be added to the current product-development life cycle. The product development team is accountable for the successful completion of the product functionality; accordingly, they must be accountable for the consequences of the decision in accepting or deferring any additional effort that arises within that product-development life cycle.

NTRs can be identified by anyone, but only added to the product-development life cycle effort by the product development team. Again, it must be in alignment with the goals of the product function being developed, which are specified in the user story.

Typically, NTRs are test requirements that the product development team had not realized when the story was being defined. The best thing about NTRs, if there are resources and time available, is that they can make a strong product deliverable within the original time frame. Many times, NTRs arise as the product is being built and new complexities or opportunities necessitate further requirements to be defined. As the product-development life cycle progresses into later stages, the opportunity to entertain NTRs become more and more restrictive compared to NTRs that occur at the beginning of the product-development life cycle.

NTRs provide an opportunity to bring the product to its purpose with full capabilities. The product development team should be encouraged to add NTRs during the product-development life cycle, as long as they deliver what they originally committed to. Remember as well, when saying a few NTRs are fine, the quality of the NTRs matters as much as quantity of NTRs generated.

A product development team may identify ten NTRs for a given product-development life cycle. And because of their nature, the development members may be able to accommodate the necessary changes and testing of all ten. QA members may also find it equally easy to absorb the NTRs into their workload. However, if fifty NTRs are added, that may be a much heavier workload, and the development and QA members of the product development team may not be able to absorb the NTRs within the remaining time of the product-development life cycle. The number of NTRs that a product development team can assimilate into the product-development life cycle is unique for each situation and would require careful consideration by the product development team as to how to best proceed.

Conversely, only one or two NTRs may be found, and their complexity may be so great that they cannot be accommodated within the product-development life cycle. Many times, these high-impact NTRs are spun off into future product development efforts, and the current product development effort may have its scope reduced to deliver what is feasible in relationship to the newly identified test requirements.

*Benefits of NTRs.* Analyzing the NTR is crucial. A positive aspect of NTR is the product development team is showing greater signs of ownership. It is taking pride in producing an outstanding product. The team understands it is better to get the product developed correctly now than to have to go back and redesign, rearchitect, and redevelop the product. When the product development team produces NTRs that are incorporated into future product features, while at the same time successfully completing their existing test requirements, then it can be stated that the *product development team is providing greater than 100 percent return on effort to develop new product functionality.*

*NTR warning flags.* There are two major warning flags that NTRs can send up to indicate when the product development team is losing efficiency. The first would be if too many NTRs are being created by the team. This is equivalent to a lumberjack spending more time sharpening his saw than cutting wood. Obviously, the team won't complete the product functionality if it's busy evaluating the impact of NTRs. When this occurs the team may need to understand that perfection is an iterative process. NTRs should be identified and, if necessary, deferred to a later opportunity so that the immediate deliverables can be met.

The second major warning flag is insufficient quality or time spent in defining test requirements.  The effort that product management or QA members of the product development team are applying to the test requirements is probably deficient or not well focused.  As a result, the team is going to lose velocity, having to add more functionality within the product-development life cycle.  Or the product development team may make the mistake of committing to a product-development life cycle that has not been sufficiently defined.  As a consequence, their estimation of the work necessary to complete the deliverable will be inaccurate.  This will also have a negative impact on the morale of the product development team since they are unable to complete the work they identified at the beginning of the product-development life cycle.

In conclusion, although beneficial to producing a strong product, NTRs can at times lead to delays in the product development team delivering product functionality.  The product development team has to look closely at all of its members for why NTRs are occurring and work hard to ensure time is spent on NTRs with high value for producing an outstanding product, as opposed to low-value or trivial test requirements.

## Defective Test Requirements (DTR)

The Defective Test Requirement (DTR) is a test requirement that represents the strongest indication of low quality from the product development team. These are test requirements that have failed during the QA members' review. To improve the effectiveness of the product development team, it is essential to search for the root cause of these defects and address them immediately. Most importantly for management is to have the product development team self-monitor. The team should look back on its efforts and determine what members of the team contributed to the DTR and take action or provide support to prevent DTRs from recurring.

There are several common causes of DTRs. First is that the engineering members failed to test the code that the test requirement was specifying. This could simply be an honest omission by the engineering members or it could be an engineering member who is either overly eager or is careless with his or her work and failed to develop and validate the test requirement. To ensure that the engineering member did indeed understand, develop, and validate the test requirement, I recommend that the engineering member initial or otherwise indicate that the test requirement was successfully validated as functional during the development phase. This promotes accountability and ownership, and leaves a clear audit trail of product development team contributions.

The second common cause of DTRs found during QA members' verification effort is a delta between the environment where the engineering member verified that the product functionality satisfied the test requirement and the environment where the QA members perform their verification. In this situation, the engineering member had done his work successfully and is not at fault.

The environment difference could be due to a configuration setting or an interface discrepancy with another system in the QA verification environment.    When this occurs, the product development team will need to investigate where the difference lies and take actions to eliminate it.

A third reason DTRs may arise during QA verification effort is due to a data anomaly.    The QA members may use different data inputs or have different data outputs than what was expected when the test requirement was defined and verified by the engineering member during development.    When this occurs there may have been a misinterpretation of the test requirement data expectations.    If so, those data expectations need to be discussed and resolved by the product development team.    Many times, although not all the time, this data differential requires an adjustment by the QA members performing the verification in order to stay within the expectations of the test requirements.    If the data being used is a valid expectation for the product functionality to perform under and it is outside the definition of the test requirement, then a NTR should be defined so the product can be enhanced to manage this new data expectation.

The DTRs that are due to environment or data deltas should be segregated out when reporting how successfully test requirements were executed in QA members' evaluations.    These defects aren't necessarily due to poor code quality generated by development members.    Failed test requirements in this category will require additional analysis to determine their root cause and to prevent their recurrence in future product-development life cycles.

## Rejected Test Requirements (RTR)

Test requirements are basically managed within the context of the user story. The user story allows the product development team to deliver specific features that are defined and required by the product owner in order to create the product.

As the product development team adds test requirements, it needs to ensure that the test requirements are within the scope and purpose of the user story. This takes discipline and sometimes consensus to determine if the test requirements align to the user story. If Test Requirements do not fulfill the user story, then the product development team is encouraged to reject the test requirement. These types of test requirements would be identified as an RTR.

The RTR is not necessarily wasted effort. Many times RTRs are great ideas that add value to the product, but they will need to be performed under a different product-development life cycle. Other times RTRs are well thought out and may be totally outside the scope of the product itself. These would certainly be discarded and considered under a subsequent project initiative.

RTRs should be tracked for two purposes. First is to transition the RTR to an existing or future user story so that the value it provides to the product can be actualized in functionality sometime in the future. The second reason to track RTRs is to provide a gauge into the efficiency and quality contribution of the product development team. If team members are generating a large number of RTRs, which many times will require discussion by the members of the product development team, then the team is losing efficiency. It is spending more effort evaluating RTRs than defining, developing, and verifying the product function for the consumer. In this situation, those product team members will need to be evaluated to see if their contributions can be optimized more effectively.

# 5. IMPLEMENTING TREDD

At this point, the basic premise and components of TREDD have been explained in detail. The goal and promise that TREDD offers to companies and teams looking to develop an outstanding product should be understood. What is left to explore is a formula for how to implement TREDD. After all, without a successful implementation, TREDD would be only an academic premise, which it is not. One of TREDD's benefits is to provide individuals the ability to develop products by leveraging not only their own talents, but to recognize that by applying their talents they can equally raise the talents of the other team members, so they realize their full potential in pursuit of developing an outstanding product.

The desire to lay forth a clear blueprint, in which a company can assemble a product development team that implements TREDD and thereby produces release after release of product features that continuously surpass the expectations of prior releases, is very tempting. With such a plan and with such a guarantee, many people would be viewed as managerial gurus, for having the ability to turn around poorly executing teams. It is all too easy to find consulting and training firms that promise to provide the services that can deliver such a formula. Unfortunately, for senior management who buy into those offers, the results are usually disappointing.

Remember, TREDD seeks to help the product development team achieve its greatest efficiency and effectiveness. This team is not a static entity. It is highly dynamic and extremely interactive. The team changes moment by moment. Its interactions between members and with those in the company always fluctuate. From one organization to the next and even within an organization, the team members are never the same. Their backgrounds, personalities, ambitions, and talents vary too greatly. Over time teams will change as members come and go. The beauty of being human is the innate attribute of dynamics. So we must recognize that we are working with people, not machines, or theorems, or formulas. As such, there is no single path to implementing TREDD. Just as a strong bridge and building can bend and yield to demanding forces, the TREDD methodology has equal strength that provides a team and organization the capability of flexibility, with strong anchors of recommended processes, procedures, and execution that allow the product development team to perform at a higher level.

It is important when implementing TREDD not to expect a single intervening action that will change the character of the product development team. Rather the company should be prepared to establish an environment in which the composite principles of the TREDD methodology can be established and thrive, and expect the product development team to evolve to greater productivity over a short period of time.

The constructs of TREDD are the touchstones for success. Like helpful rocks when crossing a stream, these touchstones provide a person traversing the stream safe and, hopefully, dry passage. Which stones to step on can vary from person to person, and even day by day depending on the height of the water. Before crossing the stream, it may not be important to determine exactly which stones to walk on. What is more important is to understand that there are sufficient stones available for the person to achieve his or her goal, and if one stone proves unstable, an alternate stone is available so the person can move ahead and achieve the end result.

Similarly, the organization implementing TREDD will need to understand the fundamentals of TREDD and have the courage to support the product development team as it applies the TREDD principles when and as it sees fit. The organization has to have managerial insight to assemble the right talent and make adjustments to the team as required in order to achieve efficient execution during product development.

Three elements—management support, product development team, and environment—will require investment by the organization in order to successfully realize the benefits of TREDD.

## Management Support

*Commitment*

It should go without saying that the product development team needs to have the support of the organization's management in order to successfully apply TREDD principles to the Agile product-development life cycle. Just as adequate management support is a major factor in the success or failure of Agile adaption, likewise management support is required for applying TREDD. It is easy for a manager to state that he or she will enlist the product development team to follow this development methodology. However, it is quite another thing for the manager to put forth the time and effort to ensure TREDD is successfully implemented.

Although not absolutely necessary, it is highly recommended that managers supporting TREDD implementation should first have a commitment to Agile. Recall that TREDD extends the Agile principles. Without management's dedication to developing the product with Agile execution, TREDD could be limited in its ability to raise the development team's effectiveness.

*Patience*

It can be said that patience is the partner to attaining success for implementing TREDD.   Implementing any new methodology requires, in most cases, a change in development philosophy and expectations.   The key word here is *change*.

Management must understand that the organization is being expected to change its operational habits, in some cases significantly.   Change is never easy, and the key element to remember is that change takes time.   And that means that management must be patient.

Being patient allows management to set realistic expectations.   The results will come after the product development team has understood, accepted, and engaged the TREDD methodology.   Once the team is engaged, it will make adjustments to its product-development life cycle to improve its efficiency.   This will take several development iterations until the team's efficiency begins to become realized.   If the product development team has the right members, the TREDD methodology will yield greater efficiency.   However, management must be aware that this will take time.

*Champion Quality*

TREDD's goal is to allow the product development team to perform at peak efficiency and produce an outstanding product over several iterations.   Efficiency is not the sole goal of TREDD.   The goal is to optimize the team's efficiency to produce a *quality* product.

Quality will be produced only through the direct contribution of the product development team. Even products produced by automation still require human intervention to measure quality at some point. Since quality is a human measurement, that measurement needs to be set by management. Company management needs to consistently reinforce the value of producing a quality product to the product development team. TREDD, as detailed earlier, provides a series of measurements that will allow management and the product development team to gauge the quality of each team member's contribution. It is up to management and the product development team to review and correctly interpret those measurements and make the necessary adjustments, with the sole purpose of improving the quality of the product development team. That in turn will lead to greater efficiency and producing a much better product.

## Support Collaboration

Always keep in mind that Agile is a team-orientated methodology. TREDD recognizes this and places a focus on creating an environment where the product development team utilizes its members' combined talents in creating a superb product. To combine those talents, the team must operate in a manner in which it can discover and utilize those talents. The synthesis of talent cannot happen in isolation. It requires interaction among product team members in order for them to build trust and understanding. This interaction must come through collaboration among the team members. Collaboration, day in and day out, allows the team to understand its strengths and weaknesses, so members can make necessary adjustments to one another's responsibilities. In that way the product continues to be produced on schedule with consistently high quality. Management can reward collaboration within the team through recognition and appreciation, thereby supporting the development of the team implementing TREDD.

Management's support of collaboration goes beyond the product development team. While the product is being produced, the team will undoubtedly require the skills and contributions of the wider organization. In support of the product development team, management should communicate that those outside the team will need to work in a collaborative manner as needed. Collaboration will allow the members of the product development team to make improvements toward delivering a quality product rooted in what they can contribute, based on their talents and experience, and not limited by their role within the team or organization.

## Managerial Courage

This last element could also be phrased, with apologies to Shakespeare, as: "To adjust or not adjust, that is the question." But really, it comes down to management keeping an intelligent eye on the product development team during each iteration, evaluating the TREDD measurements, as well as the team dynamics in determining if any changes are required for each product-development life cycle.

Changes to the team membership means that management has to address the issue of risk. Since the future is never known for certain, change carries with it the possibility of decreased efficiency or quality from the product development team. Changing members of the team should, when possible, involve the team itself. Ideally, the product development team should request the change to allow it to perform more effectively, through its desire to achieve greater quality and efficiency. If, however, the product development team cannot make the change, then management intervention may be required in order to create a better-functioning team.

Management also needs to have the courage to allow the product development team to develop its strengths through TREDD over several iterations. The pressure to produce results in a short time frame can be overwhelming for management. However, the team needs time to develop its strength through shared talent and accountability. This will not occur in one iteration. Protecting a product development team that shows consistent signs of increased collaboration, quality, and innovation in the face of external skepticism will require management support. This doesn't mean that management can put together a product development team, train them in TREDD under Agile, and walk away. To the contrary, management has a stake in the success of the team, and its most important contribution is confidence, fortitude, and courage in supporting the team to follow the TREDD methodology during product development.

## Product Development Team

After an organization's management makes the decision to commit the product development team to utilizing the TREDD methodology, it will be important that the team have the following attributes, which will allow the members to thrive and succeed under TREDD.

### Avoid the Iterative Waterfall Team

In most cases the product development team will consist of a group of individuals with specific areas of expertise, e.g., project management, business analysis, engineering, testing.  Then, as they are trained in Agile, they execute their talents in exclusive areas within a period of iterative development (two or four weeks usually).  The iteration becomes what is known as a *miniwaterfall*.  The engineers can't begin work until the business analysis finishes the requirements.  The testing members can't begin their work until engineering finishes all its development.  The SCRUM master becomes a project manager, helping define the boundaries of product development with specific dates within the iteration, when each product development subgroup will complete its deliverable.  This means that many members of the product development team will not be utilizing their talents during a good part of the iteration.

Some companies recognize this and overlap product-development life cycles.  For example, the testing for one product-development's life cycle occurs during the subsequent product-development life cycle.  On the surface, this shows that all resources are fully engaged.  However, what is really happening is that the product development team no longer is able to produce a working product at the end of a product-development life cycle.  Work is spread out over several cycles, causing a loss of focus on deliverables for each life cycle, and requiring more coordination and communication by management.  Additionally, issues that are found in testing during a given product-development life cycle overflow into the subsequent life cycle, which may eventually be corrected in a third one.  Product-development life cycles performed in this manner can produce a product. However, the efficiency of the team and its collaborative energy will be spent more on coordinating work across various product-development life cycles instead of focusing on delivering a viable product feature within a single life cycle.

The overlapping iterations, and failure to complete work committed to within an iteration, is a strong sign that the product development team is not working collaboratively, but rather in a waterfall fashion, where its talents are applied in isolation during the iteration(s).  Just as a single thread of string is weaker than several threads woven together to form a rope, the collective strength and talents of the team are not attained when working in this manner.

## Quality Focus

The core attribute that should be reinforced by management is to consistently produce a quality product and for the team to make quality contributions to its fellow members, as well as to those outside the team.  The quality focus should stem from the team members' desire to attain excellence in their own performance.  This is a key characteristic for each member.  Team members should each have a goal to reach a high level of excellence.  Teams with members who do not value excellence will clash with those who do have that desire for excellence.  Additionally, their mediocre attitude will have a negative effect on quality.

## Value Collaboration

Because the team is an organic entity, the human engagement of unselfishness and appreciation of one another's talents needs to be present and fostered in each and every iteration.  Members of the team need to be willing to challenge the status quo of most software development methodologies that promote the idea of people contributing to one and only one area of expertise.  The team members need to move beyond the traditional boundaries that limit their contributions only to their primary area of expertise, such as software engineering, testing, product management, or user-interface design.  The team that values collaboration has to see beyond these outdated boundaries, and realize that each member has the ability to contribute to the product beyond his or her normal skill set. Collaboration allows the product development team to utilize all of their collective talents in development of the product.

## Embrace Transparency

An individual's willingness to allow others to see faults and virtues of his work depends directly on self-confidence and self-security. This is equally true of the product development team. TREDD methodology provides measures and recommendations that allow the team to work with great efficiency. To achieve this, the product development team must allow its efforts to be tracked openly and honestly. If evaluation measurements are withheld by management or other team members, the team's best efficiency will not be achieved, since this information is required by the product development team to make necessary adjustments.

A strong team will have confidence that the members are all striving for the same communal goal of delivering a strong quality product. If they see transparency as a tool to help them attain greater performance through constructive feedback, enabling them to make adjustments, then transparency will most likely be embraced.

## Strive for Innovation

Innovation springs forth from creativity. The ability to move the product forward to new opportunities and efficiencies for the organization means that the product has to evolve. This evolution is achieved through innovation created and applied by the product development team. Just as each member has a strong focus on quality, each member should also have the desire to propose changes to the product or how the team is developing the product, so that innovative ideas can be realized.

Innovation is a change from the status quo. It is risk. The team members need to encourage each other to discuss new ideas, and when feasible bring those ideas to fruition. A good team will encourage innovation among its members, and likewise provide a healthy check and balance for which ideas should be attempted and which should be postponed or rejected. A team in which only one or two members are the source of all innovative concepts will not be successful in the long run. The same can be said for teams that have many innovative members but are suppressed by one or two members, who decide what ideas are to be pursued and which will not. Collaborative team evaluation of innovative propositions is a great characteristic for a strong product development team under TREDD.

## Expertise, Accountability, and Shared Talents

Each team member will have a specific area of expertise that the product development team can expect to receive contributions for. This may be analysis, software engineering, or testing. Regardless of when the time and opportunity arises, the individual will need to be accountable for that product feature under development. Each member needs to be responsible for delivering to the product his or her talents. Each member needs to be respected by the other members for this contribution. When product development team members question decisions made by other members who have expertise in a certain area, those questions should be entertained and responded to in a timely and open manner. The person with the primary area of expertise should have faith that questions are being asked in order to generate a quality product, and are not a personal challenge. Team members making contributions will also have to understand their own boundaries and not to question too far beyond their own range of understanding.  They must have faith that their team member's response is genuine and in the best interest of the product.

An additional benefit TREDD provides is recognizing that members may have knowledge and experience in areas beyond their primary zone of talent.  When possible, the team should always be willing to volunteer and engage those talents to increase the effort in developing the product.  By doing this, the team will have an outstanding opportunity to work at a high degree of efficiency.

## Environment

After a strong team that is well versed in TREDD concepts and is backed by confident and supportive management has been assembled, the next component for successful implementation of TREDD will be to ensure that the product development team has a healthy environment to develop its product.   A productive development environment is one equipped with the proper tools for the team to develop the product as quickly as possible, supporting collaboration and communication, and allowing the team to develop, track, and report test requirements throughout their Agile development iterations.

### Collaborative Tools

Recall that TREDD places a high value on collaboration.  The team will need tools that allow each member to easily and visibly define and manage test requirements.  The test requirements are the building blocks for raising the quality effort of the product development team.  Tools that allow the team to manage and report the life cycle of the test requirements is essential. When evaluating tools that will support test requirements management, the team should be involved in the process of determining whether the tool can meet its needs.  Tools that require a significant effort to enter, classify, and report the test requirement should be discouraged.  Likewise, tools that don't tie the test requirement closely to the user stories and use cases will be burdensome.  A preference should be given to a tool that integrates well with the product backlog, user story, and use cases.

Another consideration is to avoid tools that prevent, either through cost or by function, the ability of anyone within the organization from viewing the test requirements.  Limits on accessing test requirements will mean less transparency and less collaboration.  Both of those will hinder the product development team from reaching its full potential.

## Training

TREDD and Agile have simple development concepts.  Their premises are fundamental compared to many other methodologies.  Like many things in life, putting these fundamental elements into action is not always as easy as it sounds. Training is highly recommended, not only for the product development team but also for management.  Training should be available for those members of the organization who will be part of the product development team, as well as those who have managerial responsibility, direct or indirect.

If the product development team is following an Agile methodology, that training should come first.  This is necessary because TREDD builds upon the Agile concepts.  Once the team and management have a strong handle on the Agile methodology, TREDD training should commence.

Training doesn't end in the classroom.  It is highly recommended that the organization support the product development team with a TREDD coach, who can guide the team with TREDD implementation through several product development iterations. Proper coaching will ensure the team has the confidence to apply TREDD in a manner that is most effective for the team and to help keep the team from abandoning the collaborative components that will be required for them to become successful.

# 6. PUTTING TREDD IN MOTION

At this point you have been well versed on the benefits, concepts, and elements of Test Requirement Driven Development. Now it is time to synergize your understanding into motion!

If you have product development teams that are struggling with their project deliverables and are clearly missing the TREDD precepts, this is your call to action. Be willing to approach management with the dilemma your company is facing with an inefficient product development team and let them know there is a better way.

Reach out to your peers and discuss how TREDD provides a way for the team to work more collaboratively. Mention that the team's collective talents may be suppressed by members contributing only in their isolated silos of expertise.

Promote how the team and management can more accurately measure the effectiveness of product development team members through the status of test requirements. That the test requirements allow the QA members to apply their value to the product earlier in each iteration, and with it, allow all product development team members to easily and transparently make their contributions to the product feature.

Lastly, always be willing to evaluate the product development team. Ensure the members value quality and collaboration. Listen to what changes they feel are essential to help them implement TREDD. Be willing to make changes (this means courage) so that the product development team members all have a high level of commitment to quality and a desire to produce the best product in the marketplace for your company!

# BIBLIOGRAPHY

Kent, Beck (2003). *Test Driven Development: by Example.*
Boston: Pearson Education, Inc.

Larman, Craig & Vodde, Bas (2010). Acceptance Test-Driven
Development with Robot Framework.

Schwaber, Ken (2004). *Agile Project Management with Scrum.*
Redmond: Microsoft Press.

Schwaber, Ken & Beedle, Mike (2002). *Agile Project Management
with Scrum.* Upper Saddle River: Prentice Hall.

## ABOUT THE AUTHOR

Mike O'Reilly is an information technology management professional, who focuses on improving the managerial effectiveness of companies in the financial, educational, manufacturing, and engineering industries. Since 2006, Mike has implemented SCRUM for several organizations, and mentored SCRUM Masters, as well as all the disciplines that comprise the SCRUM team to work efficiently and collaboratively in order to build outstanding products.

His company, Savvy Management, LLC., is dedicated to assisting organizations improve the managerial abilities of their technical staff.

He has earned a Bachelor's degree from St. John's University and a Master's degree from Pace University. In 1992, he thru-hiked the Appalachian Trail with his wife and now resides with his wife and their three sons in New Hampshire.

www.ingramcontent.com/pod-product-compliance
Lightning Source LLC
Chambersburg PA
CBHW061032050326
40689CB00012B/2783